CAMBRIDGE INTRODUCTION TO WORLD HISTORY

GENERAL EDITOR · TREVOR CAIRNS

The Roman Army

John Wilkes

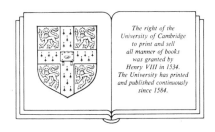

The right of the
University of Cambridge
to print and sell
all manner of books
was granted by
Henry VIII in 1534.
The University has printed
and published continuously
since 1584.

CAMBRIDGE UNIVERSITY PRESS
Cambridge
New York   Port Chester
Melbourne   Sydney

Art editors Banks and Miles
Drawings by Peter Whiteman
and Graham Humphreys
Maps by Peter Taylor
Diagrams and plans by
Alan Rhodes and Banks and Miles

Published by the Press Syndicate of the University of Cambridge
The Pitt Building, Trumpington Street, Cambridge CB2 1RP
40 West 20th Street, New York, NY 10011-4211, USA
10 Stamford Road, Oakleigh, Melbourne 3166, Australia

© Cambridge University Press 1972

Library of Congress Catalogue Card Number: 78-111136

ISBN 0 521 07243 3

First published 1972
Eighth printing 1986
Eleventh printing 1991

Type-set by Hazell, Watson and Viney Ltd
First printed in Great Britain by
Jarrold and Sons Ltd, Norwich
Reprinted in Malta by Interprint Limited

right: Trajan's column, Rome, designed by a military engineer and erected about A.D. 113. The scenes of the Dacian wars carved in a great spiral round the column are one of the most important sources of information on the Roman army. The drawings in this book are based on these scenes.

Front cover: A detachment of the Twentieth Legion advances, led by centurion and standard-bearer. These men are not actors but members of the Ermine Street Guard, who study, experiment and try to reproduce as accurately as possible the equipment and methods of the Roman army in the later first century AD.

Back cover: A *ballista*, one of the legion's 'field guns', with its crew. One legionary completes winding back the cord and checks the aim while the other places the dart in its groove.

Illustrations in this volume are reproduced by kind permission of the following:
p 3, Mansell Collection; p. 16, plan of Fendoch after Richmond and MacIntyre, Society of Antiquaries of Scotland, Edinburgh; p 16, Housesteads Fort by Alan Sorrell, Dept. of the Environment; p 17, roof tiles, Grosvenor Museum, Chester; p 17, plan of Caerleon, p 20, plan and section of Inchtuthil from G. Webster's *The Roman Army*, the author and Grosvenor Museum, Chester; p 18, Bertram Unne and Dept of the Environment; p 21, medical instruments from J. Liversidge's *Britain in the Roman Empire*; p 21, corn measure, J. E. Hedley and the Trustees of the Chesters Museum; p 24, Dorset County Museum, Dorchester; p 25, Museo Arqueologico de Barcelona, Spain; pp 5, 28, the Museum of Antiquities of the University and the Society of Antiquaries of Newcastle upon Tyne; p 40, Stadtisches Museum, Wiesbaden, Germany; pp 30, 38, 39, the British Museum; p 5, the National Museum of Wales.
Cover photographs, The Ermine Street Guard.

Contents

left: The Emperor Trajan. Trajan ruled the Roman Empire from A.D. 98 until his death in A.D. 117. He was commander-in-chief of the army. This book describes the Roman army, mainly as it was under Trajan. Sometimes you will find stories of army life which come from an earlier or later time than Trajan's. This is to add interesting detail, and things were probably similar in Trajan's time. You will see dates given for stories which come from a different period of Roman army history.

right: A modern reconstruction of a Roman legionary.

1. SOLDIERS OF THE ROMAN ARMY

The Roman army had both infantry and cavalry. Infantry are soldiers who fight on foot and cavalry those who fight on horseback.

There were two very different sorts of soldier in the Roman army. One kind was called an 'auxiliary'. Auxiliary comes from *auxilium*, which is the Latin word for 'help'. So the *auxiliaries* 'helped out' the main Roman army.

The second kind of Roman soldier was the more important. All these soldiers were divided up into groups called 'legions'. Each soldier is called a 'legionary'. The legionaries were almost all infantry.

Auxiliaries and legionaries usually worked and fought battles together.

How many men in the Roman army?

We are not sure exactly how many men there were in the Roman army, but we can make a useful guess. Here is a list.

Trajan's army had *thirty legions*.
Each legion had about 5,300 men.

The total would be	159,000	legionaries
The *emperor's guards* had	10,000	guardsmen
Auxiliary cavalry	80,000	auxiliaries
Auxiliary infantry	140,000	auxiliaries
Other troops, hired by the Romans or fighting with them from time to time. Probably around	11,000	irregular troops and allies
Rough total of the Roman army under Trajan	400,000	

Where recruits came from

The Romans divided up their empire into areas called provinces and named them after the people who lived there. The map on p. 6 shows which provinces sent most men for the army. Each province was governed by a distinguished Roman chosen by the emperor, or sometimes by the Senate.

Roman *legionaries* were all Roman citizens. Roman recruiting areas depended on how long a province had been under Roman rule. Italy herself and areas such as Southern France (Narbonensis) provided no auxiliaries (since almost everyone was a Roman citizen) and fewer legionaries as time went on. Italians provided only one man in five in Trajan's time and hardly any later on, though many joined the Praetorian Guard. The wilder border provinces found auxiliaries and then, as they settled down, legionaries. If you compare the first map with a map showing dates when Rome conquered a particular province you can see the process developing: auxiliaries, then legionaries, then no soldiers. What mattered was whether a soldier was a Roman citizen, not what part of the empire he came from or what religion or colour he was. He could be posted to any legion. Every legion used the same weapons.

In Trajan's time more and more recruits came from the province which contained the legion's base, or a region of the empire which had a similar climate and conditions. Some recruits were the sons of soldiers stationed at the base itself and had lived there all their lives. For example the Third Augustan Legion, at Lambaesis in Numidia (modern Algeria), had 77 new recruits from provinces in the middle east and Asia Minor but only one from Gaul in the colder north.

Auxiliaries were different. The first auxiliaries had been the allies the Romans made at the time when they first began to conquer the empire. They were still people from the wilder provinces in Trajan's time, and rarely Roman citizens. They always lived and fought side by side with other men from their native land. But they were not usually stationed in their homeland in case they took it into their heads to rebel against the Romans. Archers came from Syria and Arabia and since they were needed everywhere they went everywhere. The next two maps show how much auxiliaries got around.

Normally there were enough volunteers to keep the Roman armies going. But sometimes men had to be called up and were

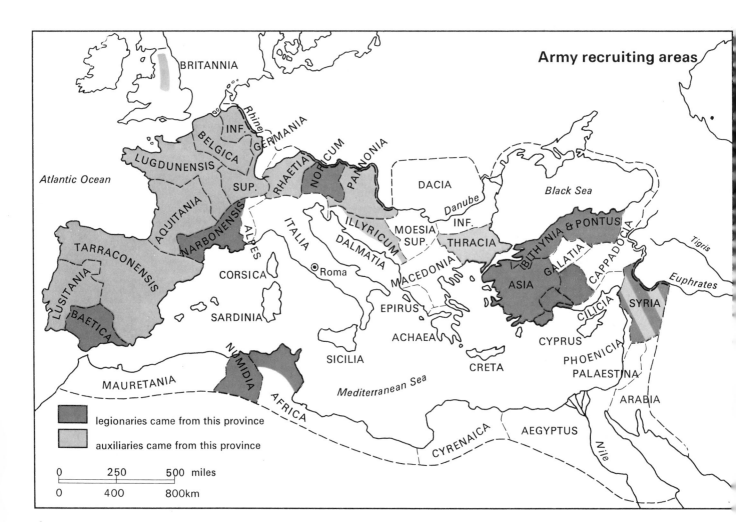

ade to go into the forces. Here is a letter from a priest in
gypt to a cavalry officer there. It dates from the fourth
entury A.D.

'Mios to his beloved brother Abinnaeus, I am writing to you
bout my wife Naomi's brother. He is a soldier's son and he
as been signed on as a soldier. If you can release him again
is a fine thing you do . . . since his mother is a widow and
as none but him. But if he must serve, please safeguard him
om going abroad with the army. May God preserve you.'

Men were sent to Britain from these countries because
their units could be spared from other frontiers, or
because they used a specialised weapon (Syrian
bowmen) or had a special skill, such as men from the
Tigris who handled barges on the geographically
similar shallows of the River Tyne.

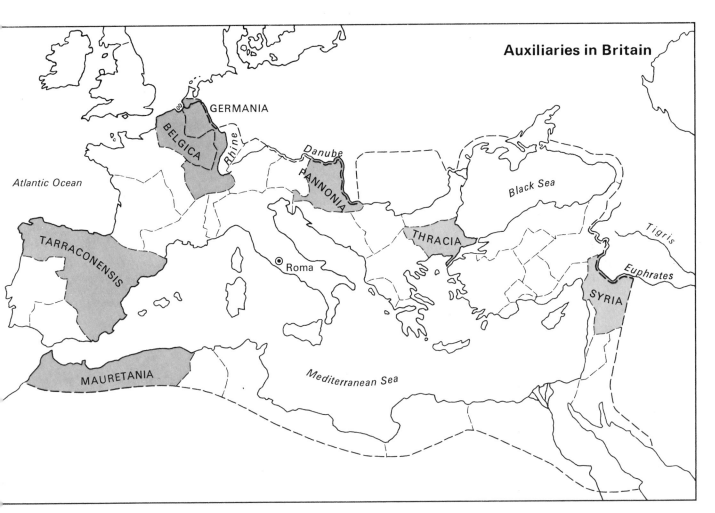

Auxiliaries in Britain

Once auxiliaries were in the army they seem to have settled down alright. They were under strict military discipline, but they were fed and looked after. Their life might have been even harder at home than it was in the army.

Most soldiers joined up when they were between eighteen and twenty-two years old. Some were younger. We know that a fourteen-year-old served with the Twentieth Legion, stationed at Chester, but soldiers of his age were very few indeed.

Roman soldiers had to swear a solemn oath when they joined the army. They promised to be faithful to the emperor, never to leave the line of battle (except to save a comrade's life) and to obey orders.

The Romans do not seem to have had basic training camp as the British army has today. Recruits were sent straight t a legion and given their kit and training when they got t camp. A recruit usually joined one of the legions stationed i or near his native province. We do not know if a young soldie had any personal choice in the matter.

In Trajan's time Britain was still a partly conquered province, unsuitable for recruiting legionaries. But some British irregular troops (numeri) were sent abroad to places shown on this map. This both took likely rebels out of their homeland and made their fighting skill useful to Rome.

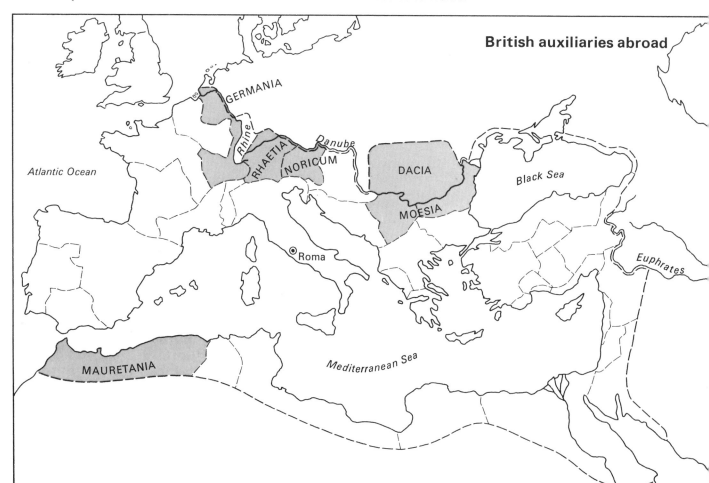

British auxiliaries abroad

Where the Roman army fought

By Trajan's time the strongest threat to Rome in the West had shifted from the Rhine to the Danube frontier. The legions moved to counter a new threat from Dacian and neighbouring peoples. In the East, Rome was consolidating her frontiers with roads and fortresses against Parthians and desert nomads.

It is easy to see from the map that trouble came from outside the Roman empire. The main job of the army was to stop tribes outside the empire from breaking through the frontier defences and attacking peaceful farms and towns.

A few countries in the empire were not very settled. The north of Britain and Wales had to be watched. There was a little trouble in the north of Spain, but the legion was really there to look after gold and lead mines in the area. Judaea was restless because its people thought that some Roman customs were against the Jewish religion. A legion was stationed in Egypt mainly to safeguard the corn grown in that country which supplied the city of Rome itself.

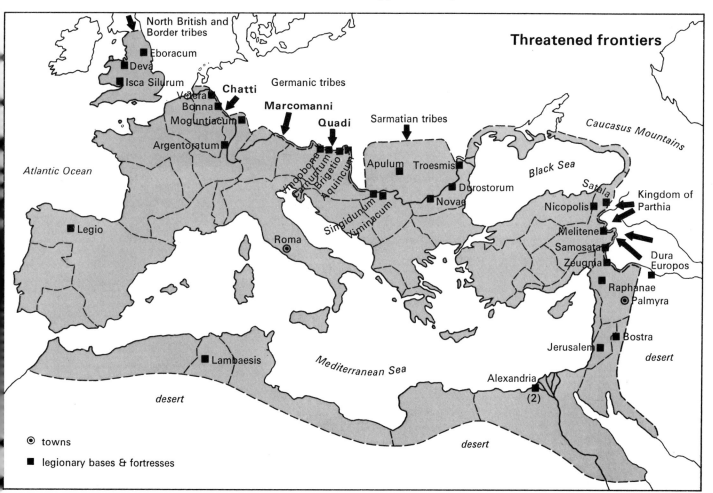

9

Bases for Roman legions were very carefully chosen. They had to be near the scene of possible trouble and within reach of supply lines. Often a great river was made the frontier of the Roman empire. The river protected Roman lands because it was difficult to cross it without being seen. Ships could come up the river to supply the legionary bases.

Trajan fought two big wars. In A.D. 106 he defeated the Dacians and took over their country. In A.D. 116 he tried to conquer the Parthians. At first he won, but he could not hold on to the lands he gained. Trajan died in A.D. 117 and Hadrian, the next emperor, did not try to make the Roman empire any bigger. Instead he made the frontier defences stronger by building walls, roads and forts.

Recruits carrying out javelin training and sword drill under the watchful eye of a centurion. As recruits they developed strength by using double-weight wooden swords and shields for practice.

2. LIVING AND WORKING IN THE ROMAN ARMY

– WITH THE LEGION

keeping things clean. They knew dirt led to disease though they did not know *why* this was so.

Publius Clodius Secundus guarded the gate and then spent some time cleaning officers' boots. Gaius Aemilius Valens had to clean the uniform of a senior officer called Helius. Then he worked in the armoury and the bath-house.

Each of the thirty legions in the Roman army was a little army on its own. Legionaries were fighting men first and foremost. But they had other jobs to do. They were builders, engineers, policemen, and sometimes civil servants as well. To do all their jobs legionaries had to be very well trained.

They *were* very well trained. The reason why the Roman army won so many battles was because of the training and discipline of its men.

New recruits hoped for glory. At first they got something different.

Romans all got up early; the legion was up and about before dawn. The men put away their straw mattresses and washed. They did not have breakfast and so were ready for morning parade in a very short time. They were inspected by an officer and given their orders for the day.

A Roman army duty-list

We have found a list written on papyrus in Egypt. The dry climate of that country had preserved it. The list comes from the time of the Emperor Domitian (A.D. 81–96). It gives ten days' duties for thirty-one men in barracks. What were these men doing nearly two thousand years ago?

Gaius Domitius Celer was doing nothing. He did nothing for nine days and then he had permission from the commanding officer to go on leave. Roman soldiers could ask for leave whenever they liked. If the commanding officer agreed they could go. We do not know how much leave was actually given.

Other men were not so lucky. Gaius Julius Valens spent his ten days digging ditches, repairing boots and then being an officer's steward. Marcus Arrius Niger did six days' cleaning and tidying the barracks. Romans were very strict about

Training the legion

What sort of training did legionary soldiers do?

Firstly they had to be physically fit. Recruits and trained soldiers all had to do running, tree felling, jumping, and, we believe, something like the modern 'assault course'. This meant going over a number of obstacles in full armour with weapons. Every month there were three eighteen-mile route marches. Legionaries had to cover this distance in a day carrying sixty pounds of equipment plus armour and weapons. The total weight was as heavy as a sack of coal. If the army was in danger a man might have to march twenty-four miles in a day and build a camp in the evening. So everyone had to be trained and fit.

Secondly soldiers had to learn drill. Roman army drill was really practice for the actual movements used in battle. Soldiers learned to march in straight lines, turn from column into line of battle, open and close ranks on the march, form square and half circle. There were also ceremonial and sentry drills, but we do not know how they were conducted, or the words of command used. The words of command and salutes used in films are just guesses. All Roman army drill had to be done perfectly, so that men would remember in battle what they learned in training.

Thirdly, recruits would learn how to handle weapons. This was the most important thing of all. The Romans made up by skill what they lacked in numbers. Training was copied from that once used in schools for gladiators, where every man had to fight for his life.

Roman legionary equipment

Here is a picture of a Roman legionary in barracks, cleaning his kit. He is wearing his linen undervest and short leather trousers, since he is serving in chilly Scotland.

On a peg on the wall he has hung his woollen tunic and underneath is his military blanket, also made from wool.

The other pegs show his armour and weapons. His scarf is worn to stop the neck of his armour cutting into his skin.

His helmet is made of bronze with an iron inner plate and a leather skull-cap to take the shock of blows. There are various types of legionary helmet, but under Trajan we think that the most common type had hinged cheek-pieces and a small peak jutting out at the front. The soldier's neck was protected by a plate curving out at the back. The helmet looks very efficient and provided it fitted tightly would have saved many a skull from being crushed. Rome's enemies often fought bareheaded.

On the third peg is a scabbard. This soldier has been given a special scabbard decorated with a medallion – perhaps presented by his commanding officer for bravery. The soldier is cleaning the sword which goes into that scabbard. It is his most important weapon, two feet long overall with a bone grip on the handle. The sword is two-edged but legionaries were taught to stab rather than cut and thrust. We can tell from skeletons whether a defender of Maiden Castle in Dorset fell to the slash of an auxiliary's long sword or the two-inch deep, deadly accurate thrust of a legionary. Constant weapon drill made the legionary an expert at his trade.

He would have been in much greater danger when stabbing without his upper-body armour, which hangs from the right hand peg. The Romans called this armour *lorica segmentata*. Armour found recently is enabling us to begin to understand how the lorica worked, although many details are not clear. We know that the shoulder pieces were buckled together so as to let the shoulders and upper arms move quite freely. The chest strips were secured by leather cords at the front and the back. The effect of this was to combine mobility with real protection against sword blows. It was the combination of aggressive sword thrusting and the safety provided by armour which helped to make the legionaries so formidable.

On the shelf is the soldier's *cingulum*, or belt. Roman sculptures show the long straps hanging down at the front. We are not sure if these were thin and for decoration, or thick leather strips, perhaps with metal plates on top, designed to let the

soldier move his legs while protecting his stomach and thighs. Perhaps archaeological finds will one day show clearly how the belt was used.

The soldier had no leg armour, so that he could move faster.

He also protected himself with his shield. We have found shields at Dura-Europos, in the East, preserved well enough to tell that they were made of laminated plywood, bound round with an iron or bronze rim and covered in tough leather. A central boss gave space for the soldier as he shifted his shield to ward off an enemy spear. The curve of the shield also had the task of deflecting blows, like a round tower on a castle.

A soldier's offensive weapons (besides his sword and dagger) included two throwing spears. Look carefully at the spears in the picture. Notice that when the spear struck an enemy shield the point and part of the thin soft iron portion would go in. But the weight of the long wooden handle and reinforced piece joining handle to blade would bend the soft iron. This made the spear drag on the ground. The enemy could not throw it back because it was bent and he could not use his shield with a seven-foot bent pole sticking out of the front. He had to discard his shield and face the armoured legionary with sword or club. Legionaries would often throw their spears and charge into close fighting before the enemy could recover.

Last but not least come the soldier's boots. The Roman army fought and marched on foot, so footwear was very important. A legionary wore sandals, like all Romans. These were specially reinforced with three-quarter inch thick leather soles and hobnails. Strips of fur were placed inside the sandals around the soldier's feet in winter. There is no doubt that Roman soldiers' boots were as comfortable as anything worn today. (By the way, the Latin name for military sandals was *caligae*. The Emperor Gaius wore them as a child, in camp with the soldiers, so he was nicknamed Caligula 'little boot'. He grew up to be a nasty piece of work.)

All members of the Roman army wore uniform. This is common amongst modern armies but was not generally done in the ancient world. Most barbarians had to pick up whatever they could from the living or the dead.

Romans had working and full-dress uniforms, with special medals, armour and decorations. They only wore the red plumes on their helmets on full-dress parades. Pictures of Trajan's army going into battle with plumes are wrong.

Measuring out the site. The master builder, a Greek civilian, shows the commanding officer how the camp will be laid out. Mensores are calculating right-angles with a groma.

Soldiers using spades and baskets begin digging a ditch.

Camps, forts and buildings

A Roman legion was much more than a collection of fighting men. The Roman people were great builders and engineers. A lot of this building was done by the army. Some building was for defence, like camps and forts, some for defence and usefulness, like roads and canals, some for the good of everyone, like aqueducts.

Every legion did so much building that it always had skilled engineers with it wherever it went. But every ordinary soldier was expected to know something about building operations.

Camps and forts were built most often. Every time an army on the march stopped for the night it built a camp. These camps were always constructed in the same way by every legion in all parts of the empire.

If a legion expected to stay in one place for some time it built a fort. Other forts were built at key points on the frontier, often near a ford or bridge, at a crossroads, near a mountain pass or harbour.

Some forts were much bigger than others. On the Emperor Hadrian's Wall, in northern England, some forts held twenty men, others over a thousand. In Trajan's time a camp for two legions, situated on the outskirts of Alexandria, held around ten thousand men. Later in the empire's history several double camps were built to house the defenders of the Danubian frontier.

Building a fort

Forts were built of stone, camps of blocks of turf and timber. The methods of building were much the same.

The first job was to find a suitable site. It had to be near water, for drinking, and, if possible, forts were built near

Cut with special tools, turf blocks from the ditch, measuring 1′×1′ 6″×6″ (30×45×15 cm), are used to make a wall. Later the turf will be replaced with stone.

Placing stakes on the wall to make an extra fence.

Much later. The turf wall is replaced with stone.

Finished stone gate tower with wooden palisades.

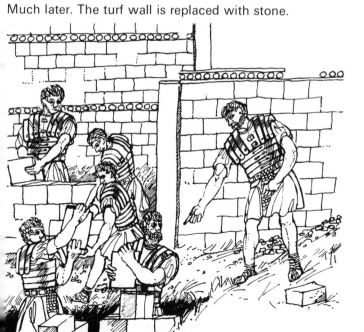

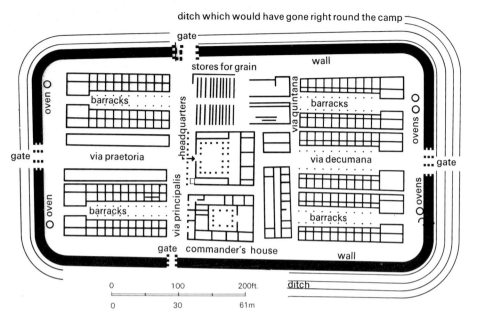

The Roman fort at Fendoch, Scotland

ditch which would have gone right round the camp

gate

wall

stores for grain

oven

barracks

via quintana

barracks

headquarters

ovens

gate

via praetoria

via decumana

gate

oven

via principalis

ovens

barracks

barracks

gate

commander's house

wall

ditch

| 0 | 100 | 200ft. |
| 0 | 30 | 61m |

The stone fort was built by Agricola, governor of Britain from A.D. 78 to 85. It housed auxiliary infantry, perhaps up to a thousand men. Notice that centurions had the two rooms on the end of each barrack block, and the camp commander a whole house for himself, servants and guests. Ordinary soldiers had about 36 square feet (11 sq. m) each. Fendoch has the usual buildings of a Roman fort, plus its own hospital.

below: Housesteads on Hadrian's Wall. The basic plan of forts was the same all over the empire.

streams for drainage. If the waterway could take boats, so much the better. The site had to be in open country so that the defenders could not be taken by surprise. The Romans were very skilful at picking the best possible site for a fort.

Inside the fort everything was laid out according to a set pattern. Each fort had granaries and workshops. A supply base would also have a large workshop for making nails, and tiles and pottery stamped with the legion's name.

Barrack blocks were built for soldiers and their equipment.

The outer room to store kit and equipment had to be large. All that men needed on active service would be stored there. This included a tent, millstones for grinding corn, armour and weapons for each man, together with his tools. Every legionary was issued with a saw, axe, sickle (for cutting corn etc.), chain, rope, spade and basket (for carrying earth). His private possessions would be in the inner room by the straw mattress he slept on.

Headquarters was placed in the middle of the fort.

The legion's commanding officer and his staff worked at headquarters. They had clerks to help them. All the pay

Legionary Barrack Block at Caerleon

The block held a century of eighty men with some spare rooms for equipment.
A 15×12 ft (4·5×3·6 m) outer room for storing kit and equipment indicated.
B 15 ft (4·5 m) square inner room sleeping eight men.
C The centurion had a whole suite of much larger rooms.

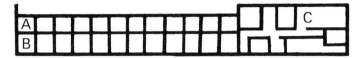

A barrack roof reconstructed from materials excavated at Chester, England home of the XX Valeria Victrix Legion, the boar emblem of which is shown on the tiles.

records and other documents of the legion were kept there. The camp temple, with the legion's standards was also in the headquarters block.

Roman roads really need a book all to themselves. They stretched all over the empire, over mountains, through tunnels, over swamps. They were built by the army. Sometimes the soldiers had slaves or local people to do the heavy digging work.

Roman roads were built *by* the army *for* the army. They ran from legionary bases to capitals of provinces and from large bases to small forts. All the empire was linked with Italy. 'All roads run to Rome', said the Romans themselves. By using the roads the army could march quickly to anywhere there was trouble. This was their main purpose, but everyone could use them as well as the soldiers. There was a stream of travellers along all the main Roman roads because they were the best way of getting from town to town. An auxiliary soldier, released hundreds of miles from his home, might *walk* home; we know this because we have found bronze certificates of discharge *issued* to auxiliaries in the army where they were stationed, but they are often *found* in the soldier's homeland.

The Roman eye for a good line for a road has never been beaten. In England many modern roads are built on top of old Roman roads. The A1 from London to Scotch Corner and the A5 from London to Shrewsbury are two such roads.

Army engineers also built aqueducts to carry water to forts and towns.

The biggest Roman engineering work in Britain is Hadrian's Wall. It was built between A.D. 122 and A.D. 128 by order of the Emperor Hadrian to mark off Roman Britain from the savage lands farther north. There are many books about the Wall that you can read. It was seventy-two miles long.

Building was hard work. The soldiers used to compete against each other to see who could build fastest. Each group marked its work with a carved stone. 'Gaius's century built this section.' Officers would come round and reward those who worked best. The soldiers liked to race each other but did not always like all their work. A soldier in Arabia was taken off building and made a clerk. He wrote home: 'I give thanks to my god Serapis and Good Fortune that while other men are labouring all day cutting stones, I, being an N.C.O., stroll about doing nothing.'

These roads were built by soldier-engineers, sometimes with local help on heavy labour. Roads were a vital part of a legion's work because they extended the civilisation as well as the power of Rome. The picture shows the foundations of a Roman road still surviving on Wheeldale Moor, North Yorks. Close packed stones would have been put on top.

Special troops of the Roman army

CLERKS were kept to deal with the paper work of the legion. There was quite a lot of this. Some men kept accounts of the soldiers' pay and the stores held by the legion. The legion always owned some land. This was let to farmers who paid rent – most likely in corn for the soldiers' bread. Other clerks dealt with letters and dispatches to the emperor. Some looked after the wills and property of soldiers killed by the enemy. Each officer had clerks together with a man who took notes on a wax block. When it was full the wax was lightly melted and the writer had a clean 'page' again.

The other Roman writing material was called papyrus. It was made from reeds. Most papyri have rotted away. But some have been preserved by the dry climate of Egypt and that is why many letters and documents mentioned in this book come from Egypt.

MUSICIANS. The Roman army did not have military bands. Musicians were used to play salutes to senior officers, but their main job was signalling orders. They had three kinds of trumpet. Musicians always marched at the head of the army. This was so that they could receive orders direct from the commander and sound the proper signal on their instruments.

MEDICAL OFFICERS. Roman soldiers were much too valuable to be allowed to die of wounds or disease. Every legion had orderlies as well as medical officers, the latter often being Greek. A medical officer's main job was getting wood and metal splinters out of wounds and sometimes cutting off an infected arm or leg. The Romans did not have our knowledge of how disease is caused, but they were good surgeons and had a useful working knowledge of drugs made from herbs. Roman soldiers were naturally healthy, because of taking so much exercise, and many seem to have recovered even from serious wounds. These cases were treated in the hospital at the legion's base.

These horns, cornua, were particularly associated with the standards, but probably also used in the field to signal troop movements.

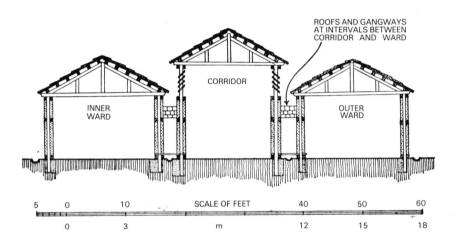

ROOFS AND GANGWAYS
AT INTERVALS BETWEEN
CORRIDOR AND WARD

INNER
WARD

CORRIDOR

OUTER
WARD

| 5 | 0 | 10 | SCALE OF FEET | 40 | 50 | 60 |
| 0 | | 3 | m | 12 | 15 | 18 |

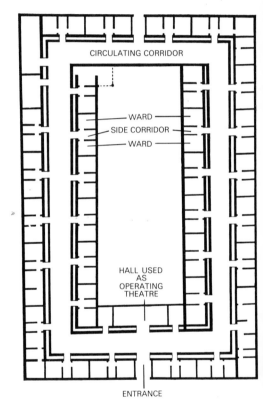

Simplified plans of the hospital at Inchtuthil in Scotland.

CIRCULATING CORRIDOR

WARD
SIDE CORRIDOR
WARD

HALL USED
AS
OPERATING
THEATRE

ENTRANCE

We have found the remains of hospital buildings at Caerleon and at Inchtuthil in Scotland. Hospitals usually had small wards of up to eight beds, with small corridors between each to keep noise (and infection) down. Many bases had a separate operating theatre but at Inchtuthil a large hall close to the main entrance served this purpose. The surgeons used specially made instruments which may have been sterilised in the small hearths found at the site. The Romans based much of their medicine on Greek practice which was far in advance of anything found after the fall of the empire.

below: Roman surgical instruments made of bronze or iron.
a. Scalpel
b. Scalpel with spoon
c. Spatula with probe
d. Flat-bladed spatula
e. Hook
f. Probably artery forceps
g. Tongue depressor
Most of these instruments were found in London.

Every Roman fort had a granary. A large base had stores enough for a whole legion for up to two years. Specialists supervised the storage, care and distribution of grain, using a corn measure like the one shown in the picture.

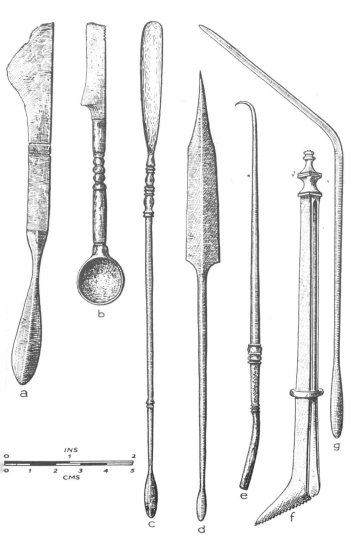

There were more than one hundred and fifty specialist appointments within a legion. Most of these were connected with a man's trade. A short list might include surveyors, ditchers, arrowsmiths, coppersmiths, blacksmiths, helmet-makers, wagon-makers, glaziers, stonecutters, butchers, and many others.

For example, some men built and maintained the ballistae, the great stone-throwers. We know one such man, Gaius Vendennius Moderatus, who, a little before Trajan's time, completed forty years service was an artilleryman and then, kept in service because of his special skill, as chief technician at the Imperial Arsenal at Rome. Others had less spectacular but equally important jobs.

Transport of baggage was essential. Each party of eight men had a mule to carry the tent and the millstones for grinding corn. Men without slaves carried their own equipment but all the legion's workshop and headquarters material went in special carts. Baggage-masters made sure that everything was properly packed and organised for safe, efficient transport.

Hadrian reviews a legion

Specialist troops, like all others, had to be trained. And this brings us back to what was said earlier: that careful training was the secret of Roman success.

We have two accounts of Roman army training written by people alive at the time. The first comes from Lambaesis in Numidia. Here the Third Augustan Legion and several auxiliary regiments were stationed to protect the province against attacks from tribesmen to the south. In A.D. 128 the Emperor Hadrian, who travelled all over the empire, inspected the camp. Afterwards Hadrian made a speech. The soldiers had his words carved on a stone pillar, which we have found.

The tough emperor said to the infantry: '. . . the building of fortifications which others would have spread over several days, you completed in a single day; you took as much time to build a wall out of heavy stones as most people take to build a wall of light, easily-handled turf. You dug a trench in a straight line in hard gravel and trimmed it smooth. When this work had been approved you went into the camp, collected rations, took up your weapons again and followed the cavalry out as if to a battle.' Hadrian was very pleased with the cavalry. 'You have done the most difficult thing of all, hurling javelins when in full armour . . . Your jumping was lively today and yesterday it was swift. If you had fallen short in anything I would have pointed it out to you, if you had done very well in something I would have said so, but in fact it was the even level of your performance which pleased me . . .'

The emperor finished: 'It is clear that my legate Catullinus takes every care . . . and has left nothing out . . . It is due to the outstanding care which Catullinus has taken that you are what you are today.'

The second account comes from a Jewish writer. His name was Josephus and at one time he thought of training a Jewish army to throw the Romans out of Judaea. So he studied the Roman army carefully. This is his verdict. 'Their battle drills are no different from the real thing. Every man works as hard at his daily training as if he was on active service. That is why they stand up so easily to the strain of battle, no pain incapacitates them, no labour wears them out, no lack of discipline upsets their line of battle. Victory over men not trained so well follows as a matter of course. It would not be far from the truth to call their drills "battles without blood", their battles "bloodstained drills".'

The real secrets of the Roman army: training; discipline; engineering skill; attention to detail.

3. ROMAN ARTILLERY

The Romans got most of their ideas on artillery from the Greeks. They knew nothing about gunpowder or other explosives. Their artillery was powered by tightened springs of rope. Almost all the peoples whom the Romans fought were not able to manufacture artillery of their own so the Romans had a useful advantage.

There were two main sorts of Roman artillery.

One kind fired arrows of various sizes. In Trajan's time the army was changing over from the older *catapulta* to the new *carroballista*, but the catapulta was very effective as you can see from this picture. Mobility was a big advantage of the carroballista. The machine was mounted on a cart pulled by two mules. It probably had a crew of eight men. There were between fifty and sixty catapultae to each legion and they may have been replaced by the same number of carroballistae. Catapultae and carroballistae were used mainly against men in the field and animals (e.g. elephants). They could lay down a barrage of hundreds of arrows, distressing the enemy while the legionaries advanced. Arrows smeared with flaming pitch and straw were also used to set wooden defences alight.

The second kind of artillery was called a *ballista*. This

These severed vertebrae were found at Maiden Castle in Dorset, England. The Second Legion stormed the fortress during the conquest of Britain. The catapulta arrow has gone right through the man's body and broken his spine.

machine threw stones and had a range of perhaps four hundred yards, throwing a fifty-pound missile. But we cannot be certain of this. Ballistae were also used against bodies of men keeping close together. A favourite Roman trick was to aim ballista stones so as to fall on the battlements of a besieged town and kill the men manning the walls. The rocks did not travel very fast and you could dodge aside – if you happened to be looking the right way at the time.

Ballistae could smash gates and lightly-built walls but did not make much impression on really solid fortresses. (The Romans used a large battering ram for that purpose.) We do not know how many men made up the crew of a ballista. There were ten ballistae to each legion. Small ballistae were carried whole on carts, larger machines were dismantled for transportation.

It was not until about the fourth century that the Roman army had separate artillerymen and a new improved pattern of stone-thrower called an *onager* (named after a wild ass which kicked up stones with its back legs).

Two views of the remains of a Roman catapult from Ampurias, Spain, probably dating from the second century B.C. These are the remains of the only Roman catapult found in Europe. All that is left is the pair of circular frames which held the ropes powering the catapult (*photographed from above in top picture*) and the beam with semi-circular slots for fitting the arrows (*lower picture*).

4. THE EMPEROR'S GUARDS

The picture shows men of the Praetorian Guard. This special body of troops was closely connected with the emperor, providing his ceremonial guards and accompanying him into battle when he decided to command an army in person. The Guard had about 10,000 men, most of whom were infantry.

The Guard was recruited from the city of Rome, and Italy. Guardsmen had higher pay and status, better conditions and a shorter length of service than ordinary legionaries.

Apart from some special forces used mainly for police and coast defence work the Guard was the only body of regular troops near Rome, the Praetorian barracks being on the outskirts of the city. Thus the Guard commander had to be carefully selected for his loyalty in case he tried to use the Guard to put pressure on the emperor. A Roman knight held this post, rather than a noble who might be tempted to seize power for himself.

5. LIVING AND WORKING IN THE ROMAN ARMY

II – THE AUXILIARIES

Auxiliaries were recruited from many parts of the empire, but usually they came from border provinces where the people had a long history of either fighting the Romans or fighting each other.

When brought into the army most auxiliaries were given proper uniform and weapons. Auxiliary infantry used a long sword whose sharp edges were designed for slashing and hacking, not stabbing like the shorter legionary sword. Auxiliaries had round or oval shields and much less armour than a legionary. They were issued with a helmet and sometimes a coat of leather or mail armour. They could move quicker and more freely than legionaries, being less heavily armoured, but they suffered more casualties in a pitched battle.

Some auxiliaries kept the weapons their people had always used. The most important of these were archers. The bow and arrow was not used by the Romans themselves. They preferred hand-to-hand fighting. They had a great deal of trouble with the Parthians and other eastern peoples who had used the bow for a thousand years before the Romans came. A whole Roman army was once led into a desert and shot to pieces by Parthian archers on horseback. The best archers came from the east, usually Syria. We know they fought in Britain – and very chilly it must have been for them. The Syrian archers were a proud fighting people. They used a short bow made of horn and steel. Their arrows were also steel tipped, and could go through all kinds of Roman armour.

Other auxiliaries used sling-shots. A Roman sling-shot was made of lead or stone. Sling-shots were deadly accurate and dangerous weapons. The story of David and Goliath is a good example of what a sling-shot can do, although David of course was Jewish, not Roman.

right: Auxiliary infantryman.

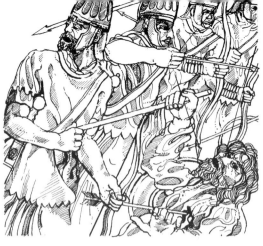

Scale armour from Great Chesters. This piece is 2·1 inches wide by 2·5 inches deep (52×63 mm).

top left: Auxiliary archers.
middle left: Slingers.
below left: Numeri.

The Romans used some auxiliaries who were not so well trained. These were called *Numeri*. The numeri were small groups of half-savage tribesmen, using their own weapons and often commanded by their own chiefs. Their orders would be given in their own language, not Latin. Numeri were used as border scouts. Romans did not think they were very valuable and tried to use them first of all when the enemy attacked.

Auxiliary infantry were organized into units of 500 and 1,000 men, divided into groups of 80. Each of these groups was commanded by an officer called a *centurion*. The officers commanding these regiments were known respectively as *praefectus* and *tribunus*.

Some regiments had both infantry and cavalry, such as the First Lusitanian Cohort. In A.D. 156 this unit included 114 mounted infantry, 363 infantry, 19 camel riders.

Like archery, fighting on horseback was something the Romans of Italy did not do very well. Almost all the cavalry they had came from the provinces. Although auxiliary cavalry was very important to the Roman army it had one drawback. Neither the Romans nor their enemies had discovered the stirrup. Consequently a Roman cavalryman had more difficulty than a mediaeval knight in controlling his horse in the thick of battle or putting all his weight behind a blow with his weapon. But cavalry could charge effectively and were also very useful for pursuing retreating infantry, for scouting and for patrols.

Cavalry units (*alae*, in Latin) were of two sizes. An *ala* of 500 men probably had sixteen squadrons of 32 men each, and its larger brother twenty-four squadrons of 42 men. The officer commanding each troop was called a *decurion* and the commander of the ala itself a *praefectus*. An ordinary cavalryman might be promoted to decurion, but never to praefectus. The praefectus of an auxiliary cavalry regiment was always very experienced. He first worked his way up to be commander of an auxiliary *infantry* regiment, then served with a legion. The very best officers were put in charge of a thousand-man regiment (the Latin name was *Ala Milliaria*). These regiments were very rare and cost a lot of money to keep up because it cost so much to supply and replace the horses.

right: Auxiliary cavalrymen.

29

Roman helmet found at Ribchester in Britain. The helmet was worn by an auxiliary cavalryman on full dress parades. Notice the face mask. Cavalry also wore white cloaks and polished armour on these parades.

A cavalryman's equipment was fairly simple. He carried three spears, for throwing and stabbing, and a long sword. He had a small oval shield, a helmet and a coat of mail or scale armour. He wore a long tunic and knee breeches. Auxiliary cavalry and infantry were dressed in more or less the same way.

The main job of cavalry in peace time was keeping law and order. Sometimes men in peaceful provinces had little to do. Here are two letters to Abinnaeus, who commanded a cavalry regiment in Egypt about A.D. 300. This was long after Trajan's time.

'Demetrius to Abinnaeus,

I wish you to know that when I was collecting corn in the village of Ibion I came across a soldier named Athenodorus who is under your command. He beat me up and beat up some other people too. He goes out drunk all the time to the corn fields and terrifies the whole village. I have written to you, sir, because I know you will summon him to the camp and see justice done.'

A little later there was some more trouble.

'Flavius Abinnaeus from Aurelius Aboul,

'. . . Eleven of my sheep were shorn in the night by certain criminals. When I investigated who sheared the sheep I heard it was Paul the soldier, one of those under your command. He named as his fellow evil-doers Peter son of Sarapion and his brother Melos, a soldier . . . P.S. Another time the same people drove off six of my pigs.'

Abinnaeus does not seem to have been a very good commander. Another regiment was much better run. This was the Palmyrene regiment at Dura-Europos, a fort on the river Euphrates. The fort was on the borders of the Roman empire and Parthia so the soldiers were better disciplined. How did they spend their time on 29 March A.D. 233? We have found a list of their duties, so we know.

Most soldiers were out gathering barley. Others escorted the food as it was brought into the fort. One man came back from guarding the governor of the province and brought letters from headquarters with him. One man went for wood for the bath-house fire. Four men had overstayed their leave. Two recruits arrived and were tall enough for the regiment. The password for the day was *Iuppiter Dolichenus sanctus*.

The daily guard of honour around the standards was changed. The new guard swore a special oath: 'We shall obey orders and at every command we shall be prepared to stand watch at the standard of our lord the emperor.'

Documents like these tell us something about the everyday life of Roman auxiliaries. But do not imagine life was always as peaceful as this. Things were much tougher on the Rhine and Danube frontiers, or in the cold, savage, far-off land of Britain, and later on the eastern frontiers themselves.

6. OFFICERS AND MEN OF THE LEGION

Ranks below centurion

After the day's march. A Roman camp.

The Latin name for a Roman legionary was *miles gregarius*. This means, roughly, 'common (private) soldier'. The name was given because the soldiers lived and fought close together, like animals in a flock. A soldier's slang name was *mulus Marianus*. He was one of General Marius's mules. The name started when the great Roman general Marius cut down the number of pack mules allowed to carry the army's baggage and equipment. The soldiers had to carry almost everything themselves.

The smallest group in a Roman legion was called a *contubernium*. This was the Latin name for eight soldiers who all lived together in one tent or barrack room. These men were all private soldiers who had to do fatigues; that is, cleaning, digging ditches, and all the other nasty jobs in the camp.

Ten groups of eight soldiers made up a *century*. This word comes from the Latin *centum*, which means 'one hundred'. So in the beginning a century had one hundred men. By Trajan's time the number in each century had dropped to eighty, but the old name was kept. In the same way the name for the officer commanding a century, centurion, was kept also. The century was a very important unit of the Roman army.

In every century there were some soldiers who had served for a very long time, or had some special job to do. These men were called *immunes*. We have a list of immunes in one century in Egypt in A.D. 87.

Armour repairer	1
Clerks	3
Cartwright	1
Senior officer's batman	1
Headquarters guard	1
Security guard	1
Spare man for general duties	1
	—
	9

We know there were forty-one men remaining in the century, but the rest of this document is lost.

A A signifer. The animal head-dress is a uniform dating back to the primitive period of Rome.
B The imaginifer, carried a silver statue of the emperor.
C The aquilifer. This was a key appointment in any legion.
D An optio. He is sometimes shown on tombstones with a long staff which may have been his badge of rank.

In peacetime some centuries might not be up to full strength. The Egyptian list given above says only forty men were present in the century. The others might be detached elsewhere, or, because Egypt was peaceful, the army might not have bothered to send fresh recruits where there was nothing much for them to do.

The junior officer of the legion was called a *tesserarius*. He got his name from the Latin word *tessera*, which means a small tile or block of wood. The password was written on the block.

So the tesserarius was responsible for getting the password from the commander and seeing that it was kept safe.

Next came the clerks, whom we have mentioned before. A soldier might transfer to be a clerk, but a clerk could not become a senior officer unless he served some time as a fighting soldier.

Then came the men who carried the standards. We think a legion had between sixty and seventy standards. There were two kinds of standard-bearer. The ordinary standard-bearer was called *signifer* ('man who carries the standard').

The chief standard-bearer of the legion carried the *Aquila* so he was called *Aquilifer*. Aquila was the Latin word for eagle and the standard had a gold or silver eagle, the badge of Rome, on top. Some eagle standards were plain, others had any decoration the legion had won, or the sign of the Zodiac for the emperor who founded the legion. The eagle standard was sacred and to lose it a terrible disgrace. On several occasions when an eagle standard had been lost the Roman army fought on for years, simply to capture it back again.

The Aquilifer is usually shown bareheaded in Roman pictures, but he had a special uniform of bearskin.

One hundred and fifty years before the time of Trajan Julius Caesar led the first Roman army to attack Britain. They got a hot reception as they neared the shore. The soldiers were afraid to jump down into deep water and face the waiting British spearmen. Then the Aquilifer of the Tenth Legion jumped down and called to his comrades either to follow him or see the standard fall into enemy hands. Straight away the soldiers forgot their fear and followed him into battle.

Standard-bearers were men chosen for coolness and common sense as well as bravery. They had to stand their ground because other soldiers looked out for the standard and tried to get close to it. This kept the army together and in order.

Standard-bearers also had another job which shows they had to be trusted. They looked after the soldiers' savings bank.

One rank above all standard-bearers (except the Aquilifer) was the *optio*. An optio who did very well was given the name *optio ad spem*. This means 'An optio hoping to be chosen'. When a vacancy appeared this man became a centurion. Centurions were the most important officers in the Roman army although not the highest in rank. To understand about centurions, and why they were important, we must first learn how a Roman legion was made up.

How a legion was made up

A Roman legion had about 5,300 men

These 5,300 men were divided into ten lots named **cohorts.**
Nine of these cohorts had 480 men each.

The 480 men in each cohort were divided into six lots called **centuries.**
Each century had 80 men.

The officer in charge of each century was called a **centurion.**

The First Cohort was the senior cohort of the legion.
It differed from the other nine cohorts in two ways:

Firstly, it had only five centuries of 80 men each;
but there were six centurions in the First Cohort.

The 'spare' centurion was the chief centurion of the legion.
His rank was **primus pilus,**
which means 'number 1 javelin', in other words, the boss.

The First Cohort was also different from the other nine because
it had 600 extra men. These were the clerks and the
specialist tradesmen of the legion. They did not usually fight
in battle, and were not divided into centuries.

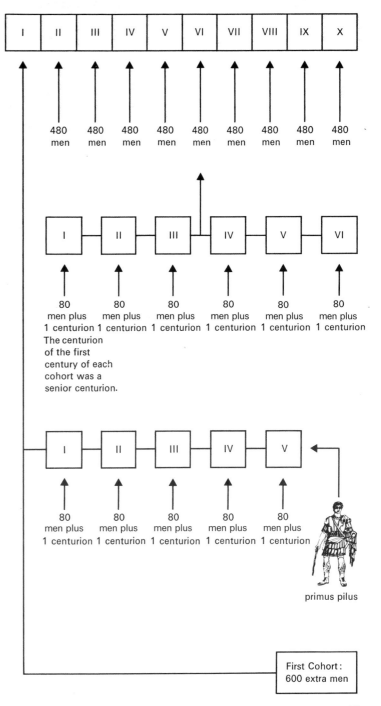

| I | II | III | IV | V | VI | VII | VIII | IX | X |

480 men — 480 men — 480 men — 480 men — 480 men — 480 men — 480 men — 480 men — 480 men

| I | II | III | IV | V | VI |

80 men plus 1 centurion (×6)

The centurion of the first century of each cohort was a senior centurion.

| I | II | III | IV | V |

80 men plus 1 centurion (×5)

primus pilus

First Cohort: 600 extra men

33

The centurion

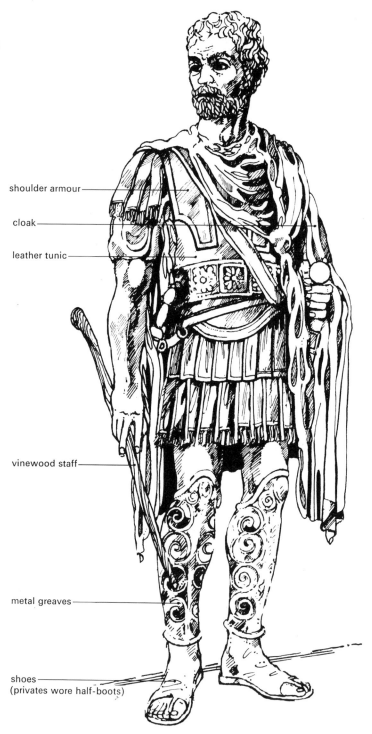

shoulder armour

cloak

leather tunic

vinewood staff

metal greaves

shoes
(privates wore half-boots)

Once made centurion a man might be promoted within th
legion or by transfer to another. This was often done. On
reason why centurions were moved about a lot was to sto
them getting too friendly with men under their command. Th
Romans thought this was bad for discipline. If a centurion wa
good at his job he might be made one of the five senio
centurions (*primi ordines*) of the legion.

The chief centurion (*primus pilus*) of the legion was a ver
important man indeed. He would be nearly sixty years of ag
by the time he got the job. He served for one year only an
then could retire from the army with a large pension.

What sort of jobs did centurions do? First, they were re
sponsible for training the men in their own centuries and lead
ing them into battle. Secondly, they had to account for all th
equipment which belonged to their century. Each centurio
had two clerks to help him keep track of everything. Thirdl
they carried out daily duties such as posting guards, makin
inspections and checking that any other work was properl
done.

The chief centurion and the senior centurions also had a ver
important job. They had all been in the army a long time
probably over thirty years. They knew all there was to kno
about fighting. They had the job of advising the commande
how he should fight his wars and battles. The Romans had
council of war before each big battle and the senior centurion
would be expected to give their opinion about the enemy an
the chances of victory.

The chief centurion himself supervised his fellow officer
and advised the commanding officer.

What sort of men were chosen to be centurions? What sor
of person would *you* choose? The Greek historian Polybiu
said that the Romans chose men who could keep cool in tim
of danger. Dare-devils were not required. Centurions had to b
trustworthy and sensible, careful about going forward, bu
never retreating without orders.

A story about a primus pilus comes from Julius Caesar's book about the war in Gaul (52 B.C.). His name was Baculus. He had had a long and brave career in the army. He was in charge of a party of wounded left behind in camp. He was wounded himself and had been too ill to eat for five days. The Germans attacked the camp. Caesar tells us what happened then: 'He walked unarmed out of his tent, borrowed weapons from the nearest soldier, and posted himself in the gateway. He was joined by the centurions of the cohort on guard, and for a time they fought together to hold the enemy's attack. Baculus was severely wounded and fainted, and the others just managed to save him by passing him back from hand to hand. The time gained by his defences gave the rest of the troops courage enough to man the walls and put up some sort of defence.'

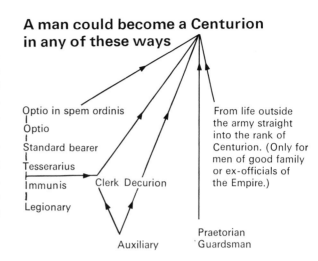

A man could become a Centurion in any of these ways

Optio in spem ordinis
Optio
Standard bearer
Tesserarius
Immunis
Legionary

Clerk   Decurion

Auxiliary

From life outside the army straight into the rank of Centurion. (Only for men of good family or ex-officials of the Empire.)

Praetorian Guardsman

Discipline in the Roman army

Centurions were the men who kept discipline in the Roman army. And the discipline was tough.

A centurion's badge was a staff made out of hard vine wood. You can see it in the pictures. It was not for ornament. The Roman historian Tacitus tells us that when the soldiers in Germany mutinied it was the centurions who were attacked first. One of them was killed. His name was Lucilius, but the soldiers had nicknamed him *Cedo Alteram*, which means 'Give me another'. This was what he shouted when he broke his stick beating a soldier. The mutineers gave the other centurions sixty blows – one for every centurion in the legion.

Other Roman army punishments were given by centurions or higher officers.

If a soldier had some small but silly fault, like being late on parade or having dirty armour, he was given the sort of punishment which made him feel a fool. He might have to stand outside headquarters all day, but without weapons or armour, to show he was not worthy to be a soldier.

More serious crimes, like sleeping on guard or deserting, were punished by flogging or being reduced in rank. In time of war the penalty would be death.

If a whole unit, such as a century or cohort, was disobedient it would be punished. It might have to camp outside the main fort. This gave the guilty soldiers extra duties. They could not sleep protected by the walls of the fort. They had to do extra guards and stay awake most of the night.

Soldiers might be put on a ration of bread made of barley instead of wheat. Again, this was a disgrace as well as a punishment – like being put on bread and water nowadays.

The most serious punishment in the army was discharge in disgrace. It was given for running away in battle or losing an eagle standard.

Before the time of Trajan, a unit which disgraced itself might be *decimated*, that is, one man in every ten would be clubbed or stoned to death by the rest of the army. But by Trajan's time this terrible punishment had died out.

Higher officers of the Roman army

A military tribune
in full dress uniform.

A legate.

The rank above chief centurion was that of *praefectus cast-rorum*. It was given to men who had been chief centurions. The camp prefect looked after equipment and building works but could command the legion when his seniors were absent.

So far we have looked at long-service officers and men. Now comes a big difference. The highest officers of the Roman army did not spend all their time as soldiers.

Above camp prefects came the military tribunes. There were six of these officers in each legion. Five of them were either young Roman nobles or older men from what was called the Equestrian Order. An equestrian military tribune was about thirty years old. He would have come up the hard way, starting as an auxiliary officer and transferring to a legion after several years' service.

Military tribunes did not have definite duties within the legion and therefore had more opportunity to learn the art of war and military administration.

The sixth military tribune was always a Roman noble. He would be a man in his early twenties. He might belong to one of the greatest families in Rome and be a personal friend of the commander of the legion. After two or three years in the army he would go back to Rome and be given a government job. If he did well and the emperor was pleased with him he might be given command of a legion later on.

Every Roman who wanted to get on had to go into the army. Some who were not very good at fighting preferred to do something else. A Roman writer called Pliny spent his time as a military tribune checking accounts to see who was cheating the government.

The commanding officer of a Roman legion was called a *legate*. Legates were always Roman nobles. A legate would be about thirty years of age. Legates were chosen by the emperor himself. It was a very important job. Rome had only thirty legions and could not afford to lose any. Also the emperor had to be careful not to choose anyone who might use his troops to start a rebellion.

Some legates might become generals with two or three legions under their command.

The Roman idea of giving the highest men in their land some knowledge of the army was good and sensible. Such men could turn their hands to anything, and when they became governors of provinces they knew about armies and wars.

There were professional officers in the Roman army but most young nobles did not make it a career for life. A young tribune or even a young legate might waste his time in the army. If he became a general he might have forgotten how to direct a battle or lead an army. Sometimes the emperor made a terrible mistake when he chose a general.

In A.D. 9 a nobleman called Quintilius Varus was sent by the Emperor Augustus to fight the Germans. He had three legions and no brains. His army was surrounded in a swampy forest and attacked at night. Almost every man was killed or captured in those few terrible hours of darkness. The Romans never conquered Germany. There is a story that Augustus used to wander through his palace in the middle of the night crying out 'Varus, Varus, give me back my three legions!'

You may be able to see now why the centurions were so important. The army was their life. High officers came and went; centurions went on for ever. So commanders depended on their advice, given in the council of war.

7. OFF DUTY

Training stopped at sunset. Having posted guards, the camp or barracks settled down to cook its evening meal. This was the main meal of the day. The soldiers had corn, made into a kind of porridge, bread, lard, soups and vegetables. Sometimes there was chicken or game like deer or boar. We eat far more butcher's meat than they did; if they had any it would be beef. They mostly drank cheap wine or vinegar and water. When a soldier gave this drink to Jesus on the Cross he was only trying to help him.

After the evening meal, soldiers not on guard were free to go out of camp. What they did off duty depended on where they were stationed. Many old cities in the east could give the soldiers the wine, women and song they looked for.

In Germany or Britain it might be a different story. Things could be dull in the bleak forts there, even though a small village sometimes grew up nearby. The soldiers mostly went to the bath-house, which was like a modern Turkish bath. This sort of bath was found all over the empire and was a social club as well as a place for washing. Legionaries spent hours there, gambling and talking.

What did they talk about? We do not know. No Roman legionary has left us a diary and we have very few personal letters or other records. But we can guess.

Perhaps they talked about money. Pay in the Roman army is difficult to explain because we cannot turn Roman money into modern money. We do not have many facts about how much the soldiers were paid or how much was deducted for food, weapons and clothing.

Here is part of a Roman soldier's pay account. It comes from the time of the Emperor Domitian and is dated A.D. 81. A little while after this Domitian increased every soldier's pay. This account comes from Egypt and the soldier was paid in drachmae, the coin of the country. It covers four months.

	Q. JULIUS PROCLUS DAMASCENUS		
Gross pay	Dr.		248
Less: Bedding		10	
Food		80	
Boots		12	
Annual dinner		20	
Burial club		—	(no stoppage at this time only)
Clothes		60	
Net pay	Dr.		66

The legion had a savings bank, kept by the standard-bearers. A new emperor always gave a cash present to every man in the army. Half of this money had to be put in the bank, but the soldier could put in or take out any other money he had.

A legionary could live on roughly two-thirds of his pay. For some this was not enough. We have a real letter from a Roman soldier to his mother. The date is not known.

'My dear mother,

I hope this finds you well. When you receive my letter I shall be much obliged if you will send me some money. I haven't got a bit left, because I have bought a donkey-cart and spent all my money. Do send me a riding coat, some oil, and above all my monthly allowance. When I was last home you promised not to leave me penniless, and now you treat me like a dog. Father came to see me the other day and left me nothing. Everybody laughs at me now, and says "His father is a soldier, his father gave him nothing." Valerius's mother sent him a pair of pants, a measure of oil, a box of food and some money. Do send me some money and don't leave me like this. Give my love to everybody at home,

Your loving son.'

We do not know whether he got his money or not.

Coins:

Trajan

Hadrian

Domitian

Some soldiers did special jobs and received pay and a half, or double pay.

Centurions lived a great deal better than ordinary soldiers. They were paid 5,000 denarii a year under Trajan. *Primi ordines* (senior centurions) had 10,000 denarii and the *primus pilus* (chief centurion) 20,000.

High officers probably had a private income from their family. Many of them were very rich indeed.

Roman soldiers were also issued with a ration of salt. The Latin word for this is *salarium*. From this we get our English word 'salary', which is another word for wages.

Perhaps the soldiers might talk about their families.

In the Roman army soldiers were not supposed to marry until their service was finished. We know that they did marry and their wives and children had to live in little villages outside the camp. Some soldiers had their mothers and mothers-in-law with them as well.

Trajan made things easier for the legionaries by allowing them to report their unofficial marriages to the legion's office where they were noted down. If a soldier was killed his wife or son would get his belongings.

Roman legionaries were citizens of the Roman empire. a soldier had married a wife who was not a citizen while he was on active service, the marriage was made legal when his service was finished. But his sons would not be citizens unless they joined the legion. This was an idea to get more recruits for the army. It was hard but it worked. We find the word *castris* on many soldiers' tombstones. This means they were the sons of soldiers and born in the settlement outside the camp.

Auxiliary soldiers were not Roman citizens, but they were given the citizenship when their twenty-five years' service was over. In *this* case their children automatically became citizens as well. Quite often auxiliaries' sons joined the legions when they were old enough.

Soldiers would certainly talk about what they would do when they left the army. Legionaries had to serve for twenty-five years. When released they were given land for a farm and a sum of money. Sometimes legionaries were made to stay longer than their twenty-five years. The Roman treasury might not have enough money to pay them their discharge grant. This caused trouble and old soldiers sometimes mutinied. Once when a Roman prince came to see them they took his hand. But instead of shaking hands they put the prince's hand in their mouths to show him they were so old they had lost all their teeth. Sometimes the government gave the old soldiers poor land. This could cause a mutiny as well.

More often the land was good. Then the government founded a special town, just for veteran soldiers and their families. This kind of town was called *colonia*. In Britain there were four of these: York, Lincoln, Colchester and Gloucester.

The Romans liked special settlements for old soldiers. Men who had spent their army lives together often wanted to spend their old age in each other's company. The Roman government liked to have towns full of disciplined, loyal ex-soldiers, in case of rebellion.

These are the sort of things that Roman soldiers did after they left the army

RANK	LENGTH OF SERVICE	JOB
Legate	3 yrs or more	??Emperor. Consul (highest office in Rome). General of a large army. Governor of a province of the empire.
Tribune	3 yrs	Working for the government in law or finance, usually in Rome itself.
Equestrian tribune	3 yrs or more	Leave the army and become governor of a small part of the empire. Work as a government tax-collector, take charge of the Imperial police or corn supply for Rome.
Camp prefect	30–40 yrs	Leave the army and do the same jobs as an equestrian tribune. Stay in the army and get the chance of commanding two legions in Egypt which belonged to the emperor himself. No noble could command them in case he rebelled and cut off the supply of Egyptian corn to Rome.
Chief centurion	30+ yrs	Leave the army. Work for the emperor as tax-collector. Buy a large farm. Become a trader. *Or* stay in the army and become camp prefect.
Centurion	30+ yrs	Leave the army, become farmer or trader. Become a city magistrate. Live in a border town and keep an eye on the local inhabitants for the government. Join the Praetorian Guard.
Legionary	25 yrs or more	Become a small farmer or tradesman.

The Roman colonia at Timgad, Algeria, founded by Trajan for retired soldiers of the Third Augustan Legion.

Auxiliaries also retired after service. Their army life was hard because they were always sent first into battle. They were paid less than legionaries and had more chance of being killed. But becoming citizens was a reward worth having. We do not know whether they received any sort of grant after their army service as well as the citizenship.

Centurions and higher officers had much better chances of doing well after they left the army. They got a much bigger sum of money when their service was over. Their higher pay also meant they could save more.

39

8. ROMAN ARMY RELIGION AND CUSTOMS

A Roman altar found at Heddernheim, Germany, showing the God Mithras killing the bull.

Roman soldiers were religious men, though in a different way from most people today. Romans had many gods and every time they conquered a country they usually added a few of its gods to their own. A person could choose which god he worshipped. Usually he worshipped the god of the country he came from, or the god of the country he went to with the army.

The chief Roman god was Jupiter. On 3 January every year, the legion had a big parade in his honour. The altar stone of the camp temple was buried and a new one put in its place. We have found a number of these stones near Hadrian's Wall.

Most soldiers worshipped the god near their camp. He might be a very little god, just ruling over a spring or forest, but this was enough. Often soldiers played safe and put up a stone to the local god and one of the Roman gods as well.

Gods were expected to work by looking after those who worshipped them. If things went right men would put up a stone thanking the god for what they thought he had done. A cavalry officer named Mucianus put up a stone thanking Silvanus (the Roman god of woods) for helping him catch a wild pig. We have found this stone near Durham. Other stones thank the gods for a man's promotion, or success in battle.

The army had some favourite gods of its own. The soldiers took them to all parts of the empire. The best known is the Persian god Mithras.

The religion of Mithras included tests of strength and courage, like being walled up in a stone coffin for a day or two. Do not think that all soldiers worshipped Mithras. Not every one wanted to put up with being tested all the time when there were plenty of easy-going gods to choose from. Perhaps one twenty men in a legion, mostly officers, would worship Mithras.

The Christian religion was growing fast at this time, but Christians in the army were very few and far between, if there were any at all.

Another Roman idea was very important for the army. They believed that a group of people who did the same job or stayed together for a long time were joined together by a kind of spirit. They called this spirit a *genius*. This is a strange idea for us. The best way to understand it is to think of a team in some sport. Players come and go but the team goes on for ever. A Roman would say the team had a *genius* who looked after its good luck and fortune.

No one could see a genius so the Romans made something which everyone could see so as to stand for it. In a house it was small statues of dead members of the family. In a legion it was the Aquila, the eagle standard. This is why there was such trouble when an eagle standard was captured by an enemy. All the legion's spirit and good fortune and reputation had gone. There was nothing left to do but discharge or transfer any men left alive after the battle because the legion was no longer alive. This is how the Romans thought of it.

No Roman wanted to be forgotten after his death. We have found many tombstones and they are very useful because a soldier's career was described on his tombstone and so we can learn about the lives of Roman soldiers.

The legion had a burial club so that the dead could be given very good funerals. Romans believed that the dead man's ghost would return and haunt them if this was not done. Roman ghosts were half-witted and nasty-tempered. No one wanted to see them coming back, squeaking and gibbering and covered with blood and wounds, which is what they were supposed to do. So the dead were sent on their way with proper respect.

The Romans thought ghosts were grey- or blue-coloured. Maybe this is what put them off when they saw the Britons covered in blue woad, waiting for them in A.D. 43.

On the march

It is a spring evening. The legions have come out of winter quarters. The summer fighting season has begun. The tribesman lies very still and watches men coming out of the forest and turning sharp left to march into the camp by the river bank. There are so many men he hopes it is all just a dream.

Already he has seen the advance party, auxiliaries armed with clubs and Syrian archers, cavalry and legionaries, all prepared to fight. They kept guard while the surveyors measured out the camp site.

Now comes a party of horsemen. Their coloured cloaks show high rank. In the centre, riding along and looking straight ahead is a face the tribesman knows; the face on a coin he stole last year. It is the Emperor Trajan himself! He is burned brown by sun and wind. His cloak is purple, his armour made for fighting not for show. The Praetorian Guard marches after the emperor and after them four hundred mounted infantry.

Will the procession never end? Here come catapultae, now more cavalry and high officers, now the eagle standards, surrounded by picked men and trumpeters.

41

Line after line of legionaries follow their standards out of the forest towards the river. Centurions march beside the ranks swinging their vine-wood staffs. A soldier talks to a friend and falls out of step. Without slowing down a centurion hits him once, very hard, on his back. The man staggers into line.

The tribesman watches servants bringing in the army's baggage, and then thousands of auxiliaries marching behind the legions. Only when the rearguard of horsemen and infantry have gone by does he run swiftly back to his horse and ride like the wind to warn his village that the Romans are coming.

The Siege

Three weeks went by and the Romans gradually pushed th tribesmen back to their main town. Everyone waited for th attack, but for two days after they had surrounded the tow the Romans built walls and ditches so that the defenders coul not get out.

At dawn on the third day everything was ready for th assault. The first storming party formed up. Ten ballista and a hundred carroballistae were lined up in front of th south wall. Squads of Syrian archers raised their small bow and waited for the order to fire. Behind them auxiliary infantr carrying scaling ladders, lined themselves up before chose parts of the wall. Everything was very still, until a singl trumpet rang out loud and clearly.

A tremendous shout rose from every part of the rampar as all the Roman army began shouting and yelling. Germa auxiliaries drummed their wooden shields with their sword Above all the noise came a great 'swoosh' as the archers an the carroballistae let go their arrows. The ballistae began car fully hurling rocks at the main gate. Lines of men ran for th walls, lifting up their ladders as they went.

The defenders smashed the ladders with stones dropped from the walls of the town. Javelins and arrows rained down on auxiliaries trying to hook their ladders on the battlements. Again and again attacks were thrown back as the battle continued all day.

Romans rarely attacked at night. Too many things could go wrong to make it worth while.

The next day the attack began again. This time the Romans tried something different. Legionaries had worked through the night to build great towers on wheels. They were crammed with men and pushed nearer and nearer to the walls. The Romans were able to shoot downwards from the towers on to the walls.

Five hundred brave defenders gathered quietly behind the main gate. It was opened quickly. They dashed out carrying barrels of pitch and tar and flaming bundles of wood. They cut their way through the Romans outside the gate and set light to the towers. More auxiliaries dashed up to throw earth on the flames. Cavalry galloped out of the town to help destroy the Roman towers.

Trajan was not idle. He immediately sent up some legionaries to help defend the towers. They had not taken part in the battle before because they were more useful doing engineering work.

Now, shoulder to shoulder, they hacked their way through the enemy to the towers, keeping them off with sword and shield while auxiliaries put out the fires and dragged the towers away. The defenders retired back into their town.

Next day the emperor ordered an all-out attack. Carroballistae fired volley after volley of tar-covered fiery arrows. The wooden defences began to catch fire. At the same time a thirty-foot long battering ram swung away steadily hitting the main gate. A few yards away a cohort locked its shields to-gether and formed a *testudo*. They looked exactly like a giant tortoise shell, which is what the word means. Protected on every side by their shields the legionaries advanced with picks and crowbars to break down a side gate.

The Romans attacked all sides of the town at once and the defenders could get no rest. A continuous stream of arrows made them keep their heads down so that they could not fire on the advancing legionaries. Every minute men were crushed by rocks from ballistae. The rocks were painted black so that it was difficult to see them coming.

But the defenders had a trick left. They brought great jars of boiling oil to the walls. Suddenly they were hurled down on the testudo below. Oil ran between the soldiers' shields, inside their armour, in to their faces and eyes. The testudo broke up like an exploding bomb. Javelins and arrows poured down in hundreds on the retreating legionaries. The tribesmen screamed in triumph.

This is where Roman discipline was vital. The centurions stood fast and began to re-form their men. Three cohorts lined up ready to stop any pursuit from the city. Others formed another testudo, even though they saw what had happened to their friends a few moments before.

On the following day it seemed as if the defenders had kept the Romans out. But suddenly they suffered a terrible blow. Every well in the city dried up. The tribesmen were terrified and imagined that the gods were angry with them and had stopped their water supply as a punishment. The Romans knew better. Ever since the siege began their engineer officers had been searching for the springs which fed the city's water supply. As soon as they were found they were dammed up and stopped. Poison was poured into what was left of the water supply. The defenders were doomed.

After two weeks the tribesmen were desperate for water. Several times they tried to break out of the town but the walls the Romans had built always stopped them. The Romans called on their enemies to surrender. They refused. The final attack began one day later.

For the past week legionaries had been tunnelling under the walls of the town. The weight of the wall was supported by heavy logs which the Romans had put in their tunnels. Wood was placed all round the logs and set on fire. Gradually the logs burned away and the wall collapsed.

Immediately two hundred carroballistae began firing at the breached wall. The legionaries ran forward under cover of this barrage and poured through the breach into the town. They went through the streets and houses killing all the men they could find, and sometimes women and children as well. Other people were rounded up to be sold as slaves.

Two days later the Roman army marched away. They left the town on fire, the smoking streets heaped with dead bodies.

The last battle

Four weeks went by. The Romans spent this time burning t₁ tribesmen's villages and destroying their crops so that the would starve. The defenders knew they would have no hop unless they could smash the invading army in one great batt₁ Rome never stopped fighting until her enemies were destroye but a great victory might gain many years of freedom a₁ *perhaps* a peace treaty.

The Romans were up and about before dawn. Auxilia cavalry keeping watch on the enemy reported that they we getting ready for a big battle. All night long the Roman sentri kept a careful watch. If they were attacked they had to sta₁ and fight. Any man who left his post was always executed. B₁ the night was quiet except for distant shouts from the tribe men's camp.

Trajan's slaves woke him up at dawn. He dressed quickl swallowed a Roman breakfast – a drink of water – and h bodyguards helped him put on his armour. At headquarte all the legates, military tribunes and senior centurions we waiting for him. He listened to the legates and chief centurio

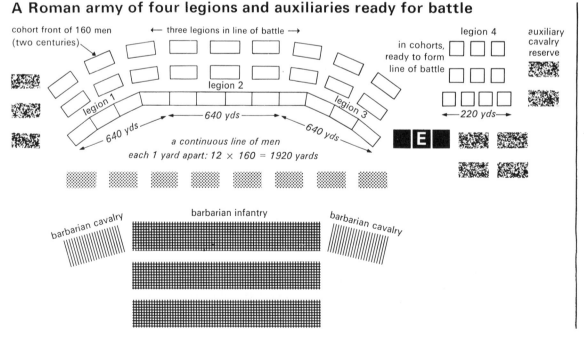

A Roman army of four legions and auxiliaries ready for battle

cohort front of 160 men (two centuries)

← three legions in line of battle →

legion 4

auxiliary cavalry reserve

in cohorts, ready to form line of battle

legion 1

legion 2

legion 3

640 yds

← 640 yds →

640 yds

← 220 yds →

a continuous line of men each 1 yard apart: 12 × 160 = 1920 yards

barbarian cavalry

barbarian infantry

barbarian cavalry

The Roman camp behin their battle line containe the wounded, sick, and tradesmen protecte by a small guard

□ legionary infantr

auxiliary infantry

auxiliary cavalry

■ Praetorian Guar

E Emperor

not to scale

d decided to fight the same sort of battle as usual. Outside ⹂re was a flash and a glitter as the soldiers took the covers off ⹂eir armour and hurried on to parade. Each century waited ⹂tside its tents until the centurion had received his orders ⹂m the legate and senior centurions. Then the men were ⹂arched off to join their cohort and their legion. The whole ⹂my (except for sentries around the camp) stood in a great ⹂lf-circle around the camp altar. Aquiliferi and other ⹂andard-bearers brought the standards close to the altar. The ⹂umpets rang out in a special salute as the Emperor Trajan ⹂me forward to sacrifice to Jupiter.

The emperor poured oil and perfume on to the sacred fire. ⹂iests dragged a white ox forward, cut its throat and opened ⹂e body to inspect the inside. Heart, liver and guts were in ⹂eir right places. The animal was healthy. The Romans would ⹂ve the gods on their side in the battle. Trajan smiled quietly; ⹂ no longer believed in such things, but the soldiers did. A ⹂eat cheer went up when they knew that the omens were ⹂od.

Then the emperor spoke to the army. 'Remember,' he said, ⹂ese men attacked the empire, killed your fellow soldiers.

Remember the testudo!' He told them that a senior officer would fight on foot in each line to see who was bravest. He finished his speech: 'Remember, to a Roman an honourable death is better than a lifetime of shame.'

The trumpets rang out three times. The announcer who stood next to the emperor, shouted out in his loud voice, 'Are you ready for war?' 'Yes,' the soldiers replied, 'We are ready for war!' Again the announcer asked them, and for a third time. Three times the answer came back. 'Yes, we are ready for war!' The trumpet sounded again and the Roman army marched out to battle.

The line halted for a moment on the rolling open country on which Trajan had chosen to fight. Immediately ahead a great cloud of dust showed the enemy position. The figures of men dancing and shouting could be seen sometimes. Women were there screaming and waving lighted torches. Others came nearer cursing the Romans and putting evil magic spells on them. Some soldiers were a little frightened because they believed in magic, but their discipline held firm and the trumpet sounded once more. The Roman army ran to form line of battle.

The tribesmen move forward bit by bit as the Roman line forms up. Then a great mob of them led by their chiefs charges forward. The auxiliaries in front of the Roman lines run forward to meet them. There is a furious fight but the tribesme[n] are too many for the Roman auxiliaries and soon sweep ov[er] them like a sea-wave rolling over a beach.

Even so the auxiliaries have slowed the tribesmen dow[n] Syrian archers and slingers fire as fast as they can at the savag[es] in front of them and then retire behind the legions to refor[m].

Now a second great wave of tribesmen surges forwar[d] passing many of their fallen comrades and running towar[ds] the waiting legionaries. The Romans stand quite still, javeli[ns] ready in their right hands. A trumpet sounds. There is on[ly] thirty yards between the fierce savages and the short stoc[k] silent Roman soldiers. Every arm is raised, javelins ready f[or] throwing. The carroballistae men stand waiting, one ma[n] crouched over the firing lever of his weapon. Again the tru[m]pet. Three thousand javelins and a hail of carroballista arro[ws] black out the sky. Hundreds of tribesmen fall screaming.

A flash of metal as the legionaries draw their swords. T[he] Aquilifer lifts his standard high. The legions rush forwa[rd] perfectly in line, one yard between each man and his neighbou[r]. As the lines meet the legion roars out its battle cry, 'Jupite[r], Jupiter!' Armoured Romans begin cutting and stabbing [at] the packed ranks of their enemies. On both sides men g[o] down and are trampled in the rush.

A centurion falls. His optio stands over him until he [is] able to stagger to his feet. Blood pours from his thigh.

The legionary medical orderlies take bandages out of the[ir] first-aid bag and help the centurion to the rear.

A steady stream of wounded is coming in to the medic[al] officers. Mostly they are cut about the legs and arms whe[re] their armour does not protect them. One man has a splint[er] from a spear deep in his body. The soldier lies quite still b[ut] his face is twisted in agony as the surgeon skilfully remov[es] the jagged wood.

Things are not going well in the front line. Heavy enem[y] reinforcements push the Romans back. The legate of the Fir[st] Legion, fighting in the front row of the battle with his men, [is] beheaded by an enemy chief's great iron sword. The younge[r] legionaries are on the left of the line and here they begin to f[all] back, panic and break up. The enemy rush through the ga[p] and try to attack the Roman line from the side. The legion[ary] Aquilifer was chosen for his coolness in time of trouble. H[e] runs back a few yards and plants his standard firmly in t[he] ground.

Other soldiers see the standard and run towards it. The line reforms, straightens out and begins to push the enemy back.

Enemy horsemen charge down on the Roman army's right-hand side. Trajan sends out his cavalry and a tremendous fight breaks out, with spears and swords.

The first Roman line is tired now. The weary soldiers fall back and the second line opens its ranks to let them pass through. It closes up again instantly as the tribesmen smash against it, clambering now over heaps of dead that litter the field. The third Roman line upsets the enemy further with a shower of javelins.

The enemy are becoming worried. They cannot break the Roman line. The emperor sees that his moment has come. He orders the Fourth Legion to move forward past his Praetorian Guard and take the enemy on its right. The legion was placed very carefully before the battle so that it could do this. The soldiers march forward behind a screen of auxiliaries and artillery arrows. Without any fuss the legion turns right. Now the tired auxiliary infantry retire behind them. The tribesmen have to face fresh troops coming from two sides at once.

The savages begin to draw back. They are tired now. All the joy of fighting has gone. The calm, terrible legionaries are slowly moving forward, cutting, stabbing, killing. The retreat begins, slowly at first and then faster as men realize their comrades are running away and begin to run too.

The moment of victory is near. Trajan himself leads the charge, his bodyguard and the Praetorian Guard around him.

Auxiliary cavalry charge forward, knee to knee as their instructors have taught them. They break up small groups of tribesmen still trying to fight. Some of their chiefs have been killed and their men stay to die with their masters. The Romans do not care about their bravery; they are coldly cut down, even if they lie wounded on the ground.

Any chiefs found alive are put in chains and led to Trajan.

The next three days are spent burying the dead and attending to the wounded. The legate of the First Legion is cremated.

Before the army leaves Trajan holds a full dress parade. Five soldiers receive medals, golden collars, metal disks; a silver spear-head goes to the chief centurion of the Second Legion. The optio who saved his centurion's life gets the highest Roman medal, called the *corona civica* ('state crown'). It is a wreath of oak leaves worn around the head. He is promoted to centurion immediately.

Two weeks later Trajan was back in Rome. He held a Triumph. He paraded through the city of Rome with a great procession of soldiers, captives in chains, and all kinds of things taken from the savages. Above his head, as his chariot drove slowly through the cheering crowds, a man held a laurel wreath, and whispered in his ear, 'Remember that you are only a man.' While this went on the prisoners he had captured were sent to the mines, or made to fight each other in the arena, while the Roman mob howled for their death. This was the Roman way.

10. CHANGES IN THE ARMY

After Trajan's time the Roman empire did not get any bigger. Hadrian, who was emperor from A.D. 117–38, went round the empire, making sure that its defences were as good as possible. Sometimes he had walls and forts built, as in Britain.

Legions stopped moving about from country to country and often stayed in the same camp for hundreds of years.

The Roman army had to change its fighting methods to deal with new and terrible invaders. Legionaries fought in groups ten deep, so that an enemy faced a hedge of long spears. Much later still, near the end of the Roman empire in the fifth century A.D. the best Roman troops were horsemen in armour. Legionaries were not important any more.

But in Trajan's time the Roman army was magnificent, highly trained, disciplined, tough and confident. The most important qualities of the Roman army were its fighting spirit and coolness in time of danger. If the Roman people lost a battle they never gave up fighting the war. They patiently re-built their army and fought again, and won.

The Romans were a hard and cruel people in many ways. Yet they kept a great empire safe over seven hundred years, and they did it with one of the finest armies the world has ever seen.

5454